ESTATE LITIGATION

Trial advocacy techniques in Canadian estate cases

JOHN HOLLANDER

A PUBLICATION OF
ADVOCACY CLUB BOOKS
EST. 2007

THE ADVOCACY CLUB BOOKS SERIES

COPYRIGHT NOTICE

Published in 2017 by John Hollander Professional Corporation, #500-265 Carling Avenue, Ottawa, Ontario, Canada K1S 2E1

ISBN 0987707590

ISBN 9780987707598

TABLE OF CONTENTS

CHAPTER 1: INTRODUCTION TO ESTATE LITIGATION

- *Introduction to estate litigation*

- *Introduction to the course*

- *The demonstration cases*

- *Introduction to the basic techniques*

ESTATE LITIGATION

This chapter introduces the basic concepts of estate litigation and the methodology of this course.

Students should have already completed the Introduction to Trial Advocacy. They should therefore be familiar with case analysis, the Rules of Civil Procedure as they apply to civil litigation, examinations of witnesses (discovery, direct and cross), mediation and submissions (opening and closing).

It should come as no surprise that all of these skills and techniques apply in estate litigation.

- As with civil trial advocacy, the basic skills required of the advocate are those of case analysis and interviewing witnesses. In this specialized application, however, there are several considerations that do not commonly apply in civil litigation. Consider these:

- In estate litigation, most of the parties know each other well and, indeed, are related to each other.

- The relationships are typically not commercial in nature, but are familial. This means that interactions are laden with emotional underpinnings that are not readily apparent to the advocates. Disputes often involve facts and events that are quite remote from the present day.

- Unlike the Rules of Civil Procedure, the rules that apply to estate litigation are custom-made for each case. In Ontario, most of the rules are contained within Rule 75, which is attached as an appendix to this handbook. It is up to the advocates and, ultimately, the court, to set out the procedures that will be undertaken in any given case.

- Estate litigation includes disputes over estates of people who have deceased, guardianship and powers of attorney involving people who are alive. In all these cases, however, the dispute usually involves the assets, liabilities, rights and obligations of people who will not physically be present in court.

- Like construction litigation, estate litigation often involves intricate analysis of the receipt and use of money. Passing of accounts closely resembles the accounting that takes place in construction cases, but with the added concern over trust-based and emotional relationships.

Estate litigation rarely gets to trial. There are many reasons for this. One of the overriding concerns is that the litigants are not dealing with their own money. Instead, they are dealing with that of the deceased or the incapable person whose affairs are being administered by a guardian or attorney. Another concern is that the motivation for the dispute is often not monetary, even where the legal issue as framed is about property or money. Once the nonmonetary issue is resolved, or once the party understands the financial consequences of litigation, the legal issue disappears. It may not be resolved, but somehow it just disappears.

INTRODUCTION TO THE COURSE

This course will present demonstration case studies, each forming the basis of exercises. Each case study deals with a situation that introduces the students to different facets of estate litigation.

One of the goals of this course is to expose students to several different procedures and techniques of estate litigation. What all of the aspects of estate litigation have in common, however, is case analysis. Each of the case studies will form the basis for exercises that start with case analysis. From there, each takes a separate path.

Depending on the case study, students will:

- Interview the parties.

- Bring a motion for directions (that typically kicks off contentious estate disputes).

- Conduct ADR (mandatory in Ottawa, Toronto and Windsor).

- Conduct examinations.

- Make submissions.

Students will act independently and in teams. Where they act in teams, each performance will be assessed separately. Students will serve as witnesses for each other's examinations, both for convenience and as a beneficial experience.

CASE STUDIES IN THE HANDBOOK

This course relies upon custom-made demonstration case studies. This handbook, however, is intended for more general application. For that reason, court decisions will form the basis for the examples and proposed exercises set out in the chapters. Each is designed to provoke analysis with respect to a distinct area of estate litigation. Each involves a dispute for which there are at least two sides, and there are at least two tenable positions advanced. Students can therefore argue for different parties. After all, the day before the case went to court, the parties on each side thought that they had a reasonable prospect of success.

Where there is a requirement for legal citation, the case study refers to the law that is relevant to the specific circumstance. It is not expected that students will conduct independent legal research.

ONTARIO-CENTRIC

The citation of the Rules is restricted to Ontario. Essentially, however, all common law jurisdictions have to grapple with the same issues to arrive at the same conclusion, an expeditious and just result. Therefore, what occurs under the Ontario Rules is analogous to what happens elsewhere.

The court decisions relied upon as case studies come from across the country. Students will observe the similarity in the way courts deal with issues, despite the differences in the provincial Rules of Civil Procedure. Indeed, courts routinely cite decisions from other provinces exactly because of that similarity.

There are several specific instances where Ontario differs from other jurisdictions. This is equally true with almost any jurisdiction one could identify. The advocacy lessons, however, prevail throughout the common-law world.

INITIAL EXPOSURE

Consider the all too common case of *Mroz v. Mroz*, 2015 ONCA 171, http://canlii.ca/t/ggqbr and at trial, 2014 ONSC 1030 (CanLII), http://canlii.ca/t/g67vf

As summarized by Justice Gillese,

An aging mother [a recent widow] *transferred title to the family home to herself and her daughter, as joint tenants. The family home was the mother's only significant asset. At the same time as she directed that the transfer be made, the*

mother executed a will in which she referred to the family home and made bequests to a number of family members. Some of the bequests were charged against the family home.

On the mother's death, how was the family home to be dealt with? Did it become part of the mother's estate and devolve in accordance with her will? Did the daughter take it outright, by right of survivorship? Or did the daughter take the property as a trustee, with an obligation to sell it and distribute the proceeds in accordance with the wishes that her mother had expressed during her lifetime?

Consider all the issues that might arise in this dispute. There are:

- Whether the testator had capacity to make the will.

- Whether the daughter exerted undue influence to cause the gift.

- Whether the testator's lawyer gave effective legal advice to the testator.

- Whether the "gift" to the daughter was effective.

- If it was effective, whether there were enforceable strings attached.

- If enforceable, which conditions attached (there were two gifts of $70,000 each, and 5 of $10,000 each).

- Whether there was misconduct by the daughter that should attract legal sanction (such as punitive damages).

All of this lies at the very heart of estate litigation. Throughout this handbook, and the estate litigation course for which it is written, readers/students will learn the techniques to:

- Gather the essential facts.

- Analyze the case to identify the issues.

- Create a story-line that best presents the case for both sides.

- Get the case before the court to establish the applicable process.

- Develop outlines to examine the witnesses.

- Conduct those examinations.

- Try to settle the case in mediation.

- Tell the story persuasively.

FURTHER READING

Introduction to Trial Advocacy was required reading for one of the sections of that course, taught in January 2015. This handbook contains chapters with respect to each of the skills and techniques required of the civil advocate. It is assumed that students in this course have practiced the techniques described in that handbook.

The Young Advocates Series (YAS), published by Irwin Law and available at the Law Library was written for law students and junior litigators. They are also available for download at www.advocacyclub.ca/handbooks.html

These are a set of seven handbooks, with an eighth in process. The subjects covered by the YAS are:

- **Interview techniques**

- **Case analysis**

- **Discovery techniques**

- **Professionalism**

- **Mediation**

- **Legal writing**

- **Examinations in civil trials**

- **Experts** (publication pending)

There is another series of handbooks published under the name Advocacy Club Books. This handbook is one of them. These are available for download at:
www.advocacyclub.ca/store/c1/Featured_Products.html

The subjects covered by these handbooks are:

- Introduction to trial advocacy

- Outlining examinations

- Estate litigation (this handbook)

Each handbook contains discrete chapters, most with examples and proposed exercises relevant to the chapter topic. Students are encouraged to refer to these handbooks for more detailed discussion than can appear in the following chapters.

CHAPTER 2: CASE ANALYSIS IN ESTATE LITIGATION

- *The context of the case is personal, not commercial.*

- *Back story covers greater time periods than the matters in issue.*

- *The contest for recognition as the "Reasonable Litigant" is more important than in many other cases.*

- *Who is the audience?*

CASE ANALYSIS IN GENERAL

To succeed in litigation, lawyers should analyze their cases. Case analysis consists of these steps:

1. Identify the issue (neutrally). Then list all of the elements that are necessary to establish the success or failure of the cause of action. Remove all those that are not necessary.

2. Restate the issue and the elements, spun from the point of view of one party.

3. Restate the issue and the elements, spun from the point of view of the other party.

This promotes efficiency. The analyst removes all reference to facts, witnesses, and legal points that do not advance the analyst's case or threaten the case of the opponent. Just because a witness has something to say does not mean that it is an essential part of the elements of the case. Note that this is especially true for estate cases.

When considering the story line, whether from the client, from the opposition, or from witnesses in general, the analyst should focus on what is essential. All other inputs, whether found in exhibits, testimony or legal argument, should be viewed in the light of that standard: is this essential?

Back story is something quite different. In cases generally, back story is necessary to set the stage (context) for the decision-maker. That is the politically correct statement. Really the purpose is to align the story with the prejudices of the audience. Consider these points:

- Is it helpful that the client the educated?

- Is it helpful that the client be seen as destitute?

- Is it helpful that the client be seen as vulnerable?

In some cases, the conclusion of whether the client is educated, destitute or vulnerable is inescapable. In those cases, counsel should spin the argument so that the conclusion is beneficial. Where the conclusion is not so obvious, counsel should consider what conclusion is more likely or more helpful to the cause. Then counsel engages in the spinning process.

CASE ANALYSIS IN ESTATE CASES

Now consider how estate cases are different. By definition, estate litigation involves the affairs of people who have died or may be incapable of managing their affairs. There is likely a guardian appointed by the court or an estate trustee or attorney appointed by the deceased or incapable person. People who are interested in the affairs of the estate are either those named in the will (usually closest family) or are the heirs (and therefore closest family) of the person. Estate litigation really is family law by another name.

The beginning of case analysis in estate cases is usually the family tree. Lawyers ask who the actors are and connect them one to the other. Mostly, this fits into the back story. Lawyers have to understand the relationship among the actors in order to anticipate positions to be taken and accommodations to be made. Contrast this with civil litigation generally. Lawyers start with what the complaint is and work back to find the facts.

Issue identification is different as well. The neutral version might well be "whether the testator/grantor had capacity to execute the will/POA". The spun version might well be "whether Mom was coerced into preferring the favored child." As Mom has died or is now incapable, the allegations are advanced and defended by competing siblings. Compare that to squabbling subcontractors on a construction site. There is a dramatic difference which impacts the presentation of the elements.

The elements of the case will be more focused on the remedy required. Most civil cases involve a simple claim for money, usually as damages. Estate cases may involve money, but rarely is it so simple. Consider these common cases:

- Attorneys and estate trustees are called to account. What did they do with the money that they managed?

- The appointment of estate trustees or attorneys is called into question. Did the deceased or incapable person have the capacity to give the grant? Is the named grantee suitable for the job?

- The entitlement of some of the family members is challenged. Is there an undeclared loan or gift? Was there undue influence involved?

The above list is hardly exhaustive of the field of estate litigation. Even so, it illustrates that the factual elements that are necessary to establish a position do not follow the simple formula of: duty of care, breach of duty, causation and damages.

It becomes a greater challenge to reduce the elements of case analysis to the target number of seven or so. There are often side issues, peripheral parties, and alternative relief claims. There are often several claiming parties, each with a different agenda.

WHO IS THE REASONABLE PARTY?

Students are taught that the law should not be focused on "what is fair", but rather "what is legal". In estate litigation, however, the party found to have caused the dispute quickly loses the upper ground. This is far more likely in estate litigation than it is in commercial litigation, or even tort litigation.

When creating the framework for case analysis, students should pay greater attention on why this party acted reasonably or unreasonably, and why this relief is fair or unfair in the circumstances. Superior courts are far more likely to act as courts of equity (as opposed to law) when it comes to estate matters. Accomplishing the intention of the testator or the grantor becomes more important than parsing the grammar of a document.

When crafting the elements of case analysis, the spin should identify each element as representing the reasonable behavior of the analyst's client or otherwise for the opposing party.

This is what litigators are trained to do: spin a case to show why their clients acted well and the opposition acted poorly.

WHO IS THE AUDIENCE?

As with all aspects of civil litigation, advocates should keep firmly in mind who they are addressing. A motion, affidavit or brief is directed at an audience. It is not always the judge. Sometimes, these documents are aimed at the opposing party, an institution (such as a corporate trustee), the mediator or some other stakeholder, actor or decision-maker.

Case analysis should reflect language that will impress the specific audience. If there are several potential audiences, the analyst should revise the language to cover all the likely bases.

Why does this matter?

When drafting the outline for an examination or an affidavit or even the grounds for a motion for directions, counsel should have firmly in mind the precise roadmap to success. Case analysis provides that roadmap. It warns the analyst of hazards, weaknesses and potential pitfalls. It should show the analyst the critical path to success.

Case study: Houston v. Houston

2012 BCCA 300 (CanLII), http://canlii.ca/t/frxxd

In this British Columbia case, the deceased granted two powers of attorney (POA), both in favor of his wife and son. The first POA was granted to both, with power to "act separately". The second named the wife as attorney, and the son as substitute attorney in the event that the wife was "unable or unwilling to act". Knowing of the second POA, the son used the first POA to sever the joint tenancy of the matrimonial home. Thus, when the husband died, half of his interest in the home devolved to his estate rather than to his widow. The Court considered whether the second POA revoked the first and, if not, whether the son was acting in his own interest (as beneficiary of the estate) or in the interests of his father. Self-dealing is generally not permitted for trustees.

As an exercise, students should each pair up with a colleague. One should create a case analysis on behalf of the son and the other on behalf of the widow. Neutrally, the case analysis could read as follows.

Issue

Whether the severance of the joint tenancy was effective. (*Note how this phrasing of the issue encompasses both of the arguments. It may be appropriate for these two arguments to these separated in the case analysis for one or both parties.*)

Elements

- The family included aged husband and wife and adult children.

- Spouses owned matrimonial home as joint tenants.

- Husband and wife each executed POA's naming each other and one son, with power to "act separately".

- Husband created a second POA in favor of wife, with son as alternate attorney, should wife be "unable or unwilling to act".

- Son registered a severance of joint tenancy on title, relying upon first POA. (*Note: the son's reasons are not objective facts and are not agreed.*)

Therefore, they do not belong in the neutral statement of the elements. They might belong in a spun version.)

- Husband died, with his interest in matrimonial home devolving to estate.

- Wife applies for order to set aside the severance, claiming to be sole surviving owner of the matrimonial home.

Further reading

Case Analysis: the critical path to persuasion

CHAPTER 3: CLIENT INTERVIEWS

- *Clients usually have a personal stake in the outcome.*

- *Client interests are often not monetary.*

- *Relationships are more significant, legal dealings less so.*

- *Many interviews may be necessary to understand the file.*

WHO IS THE CLIENT?

Except where an institutional trustee or attorney is the client, it is rare for estate lawyers to have clients who have no direct relationships with other parties. In a tort case, the plaintiff has a personal stake in that there have been damages that affect the plaintiff directly. However, it was usually not a family member who caused those damages. In a contract breach, such as a wrongful dismissal or the termination of a long-standing commercial relationship, the parties may know each other. It is not common for the parties to be related to each other.

Estate cases are all about the people and their interrelationships. This dominates the first interview with client. The lawyer has to probe into the identity of and relationships among the actors. Who sides with whom in the dispute? The answer is not always obvious. Oddly, parties may express positions that are contrary to their financial interests. This reflects that the real source of the dispute may not be financial in nature.

Estate cases are often "surrogate" cases. The person seeking advice may be doing so for another person. Examples include these:

- The child of the grantor of a power of attorney may want to get details of how the attorney came to abuse the grantor's trust. Just who is the child speaking for?

- Estate trustees deal with trusts for which the beneficiaries include other people. When someone calls the conduct of a trustee into question, just who does that "someone" speak for?

- Where the testator's capacity to make a will is attacked, who benefits if the attack succeeds?

- Where the deceased fails to protect the divorced first spouse in favor of the second spouse, it may well be the children of the two spouses who are most actively engaged in the dispute.

During the initial interview, the lawyer should establish who all the actors are (or were), or might be. Then the lawyer should establish their interrelationships and allegiances. The lawyer can truly understand the issues only after appreciating the people part of the facts.

WHAT ARE THE INTERESTS?

In most litigation, the dominant question is, "Cui bono?" Who benefits from what occurred? In estate litigation the answer is often not so obvious. One factor that plays into this is the equitable nature of the powers of the court. In the case of dependant's relief, the court has wide authority to can make such order as it deems just. The powers of the court include interference with life insurance, pensions, joint tenancies, mortgages and other contracts that may otherwise be outside the estate using traditional legal measures.[1]

When conducting the interview, lawyers should ask open questions about who the relevant actors are. Each answer should be followed up with targeted questions to determine the interests of that actor. These questions may ask about events that took place outside the arena of the dispute itself. For example, in a dispute involving how the attorney has dealt with the property of an aged parent, follow-up questions could include how that attorney dealt with the parent before receiving the power of attorney in the first place.

Case analysis is only as good as the information available. Lawyers should probe for this information beyond the areas that would normally govern the inquiry. Take the example of a case involving the parent's testamentary decision to give the family business to all of the children, instead of to

---

[1] Succession Law Reform Act, Part V.

the child most actively involved in that business. The aggrieved child complains that there was a promise to exchange ownership of the business for many years of unpaid or underpaid work. The lawyer should ask about the role of the other children in the business as well as the opportunities foregone by the complaining child. Do any of the siblings side with the partner-child? The answers may not be relevant to the testator's decision, but how does the lawyer know without asking?

THE SIGNIFICANCE OF RELATIONSHIPS

Family members often form allegiances years before the events that gave rise to the present dispute. Often, but not always, these inform the positions taken during the dispute. The fact that the testator leaves behind a spouse, siblings, children and grandchildren does not tell the lawyer who is allied with whom. Animosities within a family may dictate positions taken, and the strength of those positions.

Experienced estate litigators can recite anecdotes of family disputes involving legally trivial matters that led to lengthy and costly litigation. Who gets the family photos may be more important than who gets the stock portfolio. The parties may not be able to fight over the family photos, and so they beat each other up over the stock portfolio. At mediation, they agree to share the photos and suddenly the stock portfolio becomes a backwater that is resolved instantly.

If all of this appears to resemble family law more so than it does other aspects of civil litigation, estate practitioners can confirm that this is, indeed, the case. It is necessary for estate lawyers to understand family law, because the rights of the parties often depend upon what the family law dictates at the time of the dispute or at the time of the decision that led to the dispute.

Consider the right of the surviving spouse to elect net division of family assets instead of what is granted in the will or under an intestacy.[2] Without a full understanding of this part of the family law, how can the estate lawyer advise one of the parties to a dispute involving a spouse?

The court may not ask about the testator's reasons for a specific disposition in a will. After the court has determined that the testator had capacity and was acting independently, such reasons may be legally irrelevant. However, they may be highly probative when considering transactions that occurred leading up to the decision, or leading up to the death of the testator. For example, one child continues to live in the parent's house contributing to the care of the aged parent. What was the intention of the testator when leaving that child a greater share than is given to the other children? While the court may not be able to interfere with the gift in the will, the court might interfere with other transactions in the nature of *inter vivos* gifts and questionable transfers.

---

[2] Family Law Act, s. 6

THE VALUE OF ASKING THE "HARD QUESTIONS"

Clients may not volunteer all the relevant information. Lawyers should watch for gaps in the story. They should ask the tough question about why the client acted in this way. They can be sure that someone will pose that question later. Clients may be ashamed of something, or want to pretend it never occurred. Lawyers should confront the client as soon as possible with the facts. They can then determine how well the client will stand up to cross-examination later.

The answers may show the lawyer a different path to follow in dealing with others. The answers may also suggest to the client that the case is not as strong as the client thought coming to the office that day.

It is better that clients hear the advice, even if they don't like it. And the sooner, the better.

IT'S RARELY "ONE AND DONE"

The initial interview may accomplish a great deal in the lawyer's education about who did what to whom. Over the course of several interviews, the lawyer will learn more about the attitudes of the actors and their relative abilities. For example, a client who appears to be both articulate and confident in the lawyer's office may lose all composure when confronted by another relative's accusations. The lawyer should look for explanations. Most will be found in the historical relationships.

Estate litigation promotes repeat interviews. At the initial interview, the lawyer deals with the retainer and the facts of the dispute. Further interviews are necessary to prepare the affidavits, prepare for and attend at mediation and examinations. These events are far more frequent in estate cases than they are in general civil litigation. Lawyers often ask the rhetorical question, "Why is AB acting this way?" In estate litigation, this is often not rhetorical. The question probes the motivation of AB and the client's familiarity with AB as well as other related actors.

The lawyer wants to understand how all of the relevant actors think to the greatest extent possible. The understanding deepens over time as the lawyer is able to perceive attitudes and behaviors during the several steps of estate litigation.

The steps of litigation also promote meetings between lawyers. So long as the lawyers are collegial, they may find that they are teammates with a common goal to reduce friction and focus on the dispute without distractions. The example of the family photos above demonstrates how distractions can dominate disputes. Most lawyers would agree that settlement benefits everybody and that litigation is rarely an effective method of dispute resolution. They should work with each other to accomplish the settlement, which often requires reduction of distrust and suspicion. "Full disclosure" often includes a discussion of events and issues that are only marginally relevant.

Why does this matter?

The primary source of information for the lawyer is the client, together with the client's immediate support group. Interview techniques are discussed in the ***Interview Techniques*** handbook in the Young Advocates Series and in ***Introduction to Trial Advocacy***. The application to estate law requires that lawyers think with a family law frame of mind rather than with a commercial contract or tort one.

With the right approach, estate lawyers can accomplish a great deal, both to advance the interests of their clients and to reduce the likelihood or impact of litigation.

Case study: Graham v. Bonnycastle

2004 ABCA 270 (CanLII), http://canlii.ca/t/1hq66

In this Alberta case, the deceased suffered from physical ailments and early Alzheimer's. He determined to marry and prepare a new will. His accountant referred the deceased to a lawyer unfamiliar with him. The new will benefited the second wife at the expense of the children of the deceased. The children and widow engaged in litigation which resulted in a settlement, but no order that determined either testamentary capacity or capacity to remarry. The children then sued the lawyer who prepared the new will.

This case illustrates the difficulties facing a lawyer who takes instructions from a client with substantial health issues. As an exercise, students should pair up and interview each other, one taking the role of testator and the other the role of the lawyer taking instructions to prepare a will. Assume the facts that are disclosed in the decision and make up any other facts necessary. Knowing that a lawsuit is possible (although facing the legal obstacle described in the decision), what steps should be taken from among the following possibilities:

- Conduct an independent capacity assessment by a neuropsychologist?

- Ensure that there are two or more meetings for instructions?

- Enlist the assistance of an experienced wills and estates colleague to sit in on all meetings and to review the will?

- Review medical records and speak with doctors or psychologists familiar with the client?

- Record the instructions from the client with video or audio technology?

Further reading

The Art of the Interview: how lawyers talk with clients

CHAPTER 4: MOTIONS FOR DIRECTIONS

- *The default procedure for all Ontario estates litigation is Rule 75.*

- *Starts with a motion to set the rules of engagement.*

- *Unlike civil litigation, one size does not fit all cases.*

THE DEFAULT PROCESS

In civil litigation, the Rules set out two default processes: statement of claim and notice of application. Estate cases, including contests involving guardianship and powers of attorney, have their own default procedure. This starts with the motion for directions.[3]

In some cases, the motion starts the legal proceedings. In such event, the motion has to create a title of proceedings and open a court file. The party bringing the motion must therefore start the process with a notice of application. In many cases, however, there already exists a legal proceeding. Examples include: an application for appointment of estate trustee and an application to pass accounts by a guardian or attorney. In these cases, the motion for directions could use that court file number.

---

[3] Rule 75.06

In civil procedure, a notice of application follows the steps set out in Rule 38. The respondents who were served may file a notice of appearance and engage in the process as dictated by that Rule. In estate litigation, the parties create their own process. The only requirement, applicable in Ottawa, Toronto and Windsor, is that the parties conduct mediation. Given that estate litigation is highly suited to the mediation process, it should be mandatory for all cases.

The Rule that governs motions for directions permits the court to establish:

- What issues are to be decided.

- Who are to be the parties (and what role they shall play).

- What procedures should be followed to bring the case to court "in a summary fashion".

Although the Rule appears to favor some form of summary process, in practice this does not occur. Lawyers are more comfortable with fixed timetables and procedures. It is they, and not the court, that dictates the terms of the order for directions. Virtually all such orders are crafted on the consent of the parties. If there is a point of disagreement, that becomes the focus of a contested motion hearing.

TYPICAL RULES OF ENGAGEMENT

Just as with civil procedure, orders for directions have to deal with:

- Allowing the parties to express their position, by some form of pleading.

- Exchanging relevant documents, such that no party is taken by surprise.

- Conducting appropriate examinations, whether of parties or non-parties. The lawyer who attended to execute the will of the deceased testator is usually not a party to the application, but is often an important witness. How shall such lawyer be examined? How will the lawyer's file be produced and inspected? Who pays the costs?

- Alternate dispute resolution, both in the form of mandatory mediation and a pretrial conference.

- It is not mandatory to set the issues for trial at this stage. Until the other procedures are completed, it may be premature to determine what a trial judge will have to do. Further, for those regions fortunate to have them, case management masters make excellent decision-makers in estate cases. An order directing a reference to a master for trial of an issue is an expeditious method to accomplish justice at the best cost.

All of the above can be accomplished in an order for directions given on motion or application (as the case may be). Where there is a contested passing of accounts, often the motion for directions identifies the specific issues within the accounts that the parties are contesting. In such case, the process resembles the Scott Schedule[4] that is commonplace in construction litigation. The parties identify the specific items in issue, together with the relevant documents and applicable positions of the parties. In some cases, not all parties contest all items in issue.

The purpose of the order for directions is to get the parties focused on dealing with their dispute. Timetables are always a good idea. Lawyers for all participating parties should ask themselves this question: what do I need in order to recommend an appropriate settlement? If they think of their own position and also that the other parties, the process becomes clear. It becomes unusual for parties to bicker over process so long as they empathize with the other parties. In this respect, lawyers are teammates. They are all trying to accomplish the same goal, which is to arm the parties with sufficient information to make an informed decision. This decision will accommodate all interests, to the extent possible, only if it is based upon full disclosure.

Consider the animosity that arises when one party suspects another of withholding important information. Unlike most civil litigation, the parties continue to have a relationship. Who attends the family dinner at Christmas is usually not an issue in construction, employment and car accident cases. Lawyers should be mindful that even where the parties have severed all current connections, they usually

---

[4] http://www.rcsolicitors.co.uk/construction-matters/scott-schedules.htm has a British example of the construction application of this procedure. This is easily adapted to accounting disputes in estate cases.

have other relatives with whom the relationships will persist and endure for years to come.

ONE SIZE DOES NOT FIT ALL

Estate cases all have unique attributes. This is because the families are themselves unique. While experienced estate lawyers will say that they have seen it all before, the fact is that they have not. Experience allows lawyers to anticipate and recommend steps to reduce friction. Even so, estate lawyers routinely encounter novel situations that beg for novel solutions.

It is common for the order for directions to represent an interim procedure. The parties agree to the terms of disclosure of information (both documentary and examination of witnesses) after which time they will reconvene to discuss the next steps. For one reason, the disclosure may identify other parties. For another, the position of one or more parties may change based upon what is then disclosed. Often, disclosure leads to settlement of some issues. For example, one party suspects that another party has abused a trust by misusing money or other property. After full disclosure, the other parties become satisfied that this suspicion is misplaced. That chapter of the dispute may be closed.

Courts prefer there to be an "end game" set out in the order. Even where the parties craft an interim solution, there should be a specific timetable provision to re-attend to update the order for directions to accommodate the events that have taken place in the interim.

One provision of an order for directions that can relieve mutual suspicion and distrust is the appointment of an estate trustee during litigation. In such case, one of the parties can be given interim authority to operate the estate until further order. It is possible, although not common, for the parties to agree upon a professional trustee, such as an accountant or lawyer or even an institutional trustee, to serve in that capacity. This is very expensive, but the costs can be trivial in comparison to the damage done to an estate through improper management.

While on the subject of costs, it bears stating and repeating that all fees and disbursements that arise in estate litigation fall within the jurisdiction of the court to fix, to allocate and to attribute. It is increasingly common for the party who causes the litigation to be ordered to compensate the others for the cost consequences thereof.

POWERS OF A MASTER OR JUDGE

Counsel should be mindful of who can do what. If a master is available, that is the appropriate judicial officer to make most orders for directions. However, masters do not have some powers. For example, they cannot grant injunctive relief and they cannot appoint estate trustees.

If the request for directions commences by a notice of application, this must be brought before a judge, at least on its face. It is common for the application to be shelved immediately by consent adjournment, and the party who commences the application to bring a motion for directions to the master. Effectively the notice of application creates a title of proceedings, identifies the initial parties and their roles (as an applicant or as a respondent), and little else.

THE ROLE OF ADVOCACY IN A MOTION FOR DIRECTIONS

The party who brings a motion wants to display reasonableness at this stage. The judge (or master) does not have enough information upon which to lean towards one party or another. The one who brings the motion should therefore keep things as neutral as possible. Spin will come later.

There is one place in the motion where spin is important, and that is framing the issues. Especially where the party who brings the motion expects some of the other parties to level counter-accusations, how the issues are framed in the order for directions can have a serious impact on the outcome.

Elsewhere, the affidavit in support of the motion or application should state the issues and facts as neutrally as possible. Adjectives, adverbs and pejorative language have no place in the motion record. It is rare, indeed, for the motion for directions to be a contentious point in the litigation. That will come later. Counsel who frame the motion record as an outright attack risk the wrath of the court and loss of momentum towards the settlement that everybody should understand is in their interests.

Why does this matter?

The motion for directions sets the tone for the dispute.
Estate litigation has enough friction without lawyers adding
fuel to the flames. A carefully crafted motion for directions
involves the court and the opposing lawyer as parts of the
team whose task it is to resolve that dispute. The parties
have to live with one another after the resolution.

To be practical, virtually all estate cases settle long before
trial. If the lawyers act in a professionally correct manner,
the case should settle sooner rather than later. The motion
for directions is an important tool to accomplish that
socially acceptable goal.

CASE STUDIES: *LONGTIN V. LONGTIN ESTATE* AND *DUFFUS V. WHITE ESTATE*

Longtin v. Longtin Estate, 2007 CanLII 15477 (ON SC),
http://canlii.ca/t/1rc3g

In this Ontario case, the testator was on his deathbed when
he attended before a lawyer to execute a new will. The
nephews and nieces applied for directions to determine
whether the deceased had capacity to make that will. The
brother of the deceased opposed the motion for directions
because there was no merit to the underlying ground for the
application, which was the allegation of incapacity. The
Court had to determine the standard for denial of an
application for directions.

This decision is instructive in that it discusses both the standard and what should go into an order.

As an exercise, students should draft both the claim for relief and the grounds that would be set out in a motion (or application) for directions. Both the claim for relief and the grounds should be stated as neutrally as possible, keeping in mind that the nephews and nieces and brother still have to live as relatives of each other.

Duffus v. White Estate, 2005 SKQB 321 (CanLII), http://canlii.ca/t/1l76k

In this Saskatchewan case, the estate trustee failed to defend an application by the widow (second wife) for dependent's relief. The widow obtained default judgment after foot-dragging by the estate. When the widow tried to enforce the judgment, the estate trustee moved to set the judgment aside.

Although not a motion for directions, the Court allowed the motion but on strict terms. These terms amounted to an order for directions.

This decision is instructive in that it reviews what the moving party and opposing party had to establish in their affidavits. The moving party cast aspersions on the ethics of the lawyer for the widow, and this was considered to be both a distraction and unfounded. Counsel should be careful to stick to the matters in issue and avoid collateral attacks during the lead up to an argument of a motion for directions.

Further reading

Introduction to Trial Advocacy

CHAPTER 5: WHO ARE THE PARTIES?

- *Governed by Rule 75.*

- *"All persons having a financial interest" usually means relevant family.*

- *Submission of rights.*

- *How to draw the lines of battle.*

RULE 75

The Rules set out the procedural rights and obligations of the parties. In the case of estate litigation, it is not the common law which identifies the parties but rather the "interests" of the potential parties. Both Rules 74 and 75 use the words "financial interest" to define who may qualify to intervene, take action or demand inclusion in the court proceeding.

This is not an issue in most non-estate litigation. If AB broke a contract with CD, then those are the parties. How difficult is that? If AB writes a will naming CD and EF, but not naming GH, then a dispute involving the will may or may not involve those three surviving people. Therefore, the Rule identifies that the usual "parties" are those who have a "financial interest" in the outcome.

During the motion/application for directions, a specific provision can be made to identify who the parties are and what roles they should play. The Rule specifically provides that one or more should serve the role of either plaintiff or defendant. Of course, there can be litigation with nobody serving either role, as a dispute involving the interpretation of the document (e.g. a will) may have no obvious plaintiff or defendant. In that case, the estate trustee submits the will to the court for a ruling on what it means. Different parties then take positions based on the impact of the possible outcomes.

Where there is an estate trustee, it is unusual that the trustee have any stake in the outcome. Of course, the trustee may also be an interested party by reason of another relationship. Trustees can be beneficiaries, for example. If the trustee (or guardian or attorney) is being called to account, as in a contested passing of accounts or breach of trust claim, that trustee is clearly an interested party.

FINANCIAL INTEREST

What is a "financial interest" as meant by the Rule? The simple answer is that it is usually obvious who has such an interest. In a will contestation, anybody who participates in the trust or who would benefit or suffer depending upon the outcome would have such a financial interest. One could imagine three common outcomes:

- The will is upheld and declared valid.

- The will is declared invalid, resulting in intestacy.

- The will is declared invalid, resulting in the restoration of a previous will.

By making a list of who participates in each of the three outcomes, the parties are named.

Because estate cases involve trusts, the beneficiaries have a say in who will administer the trust and who has to account along the way. This increases the names of possible parties with a financial interest.

There are a number of events that occur during the administration of an estate that do not involve property or money. Where and how are the remains of the deceased dealt with? What bank does the estate use? How often does the trustee account, and in what detail? These can be highly contentious issues. While the estate trustee has the legal power to decide them, experienced estate lawyers can point to several cases where the use of these powers led to far-reaching financial consequences.

During the initial interview, the lawyer for anyone raising an estate issue should keep a careful lookout for potential parties.

SUBMISSION OF RIGHTS

Rule 75.07 specifically allows people who have a financial interest to "submit" their rights to court. This means that they are not parties to the proceeding. They will not be served with written notice of anything, except the hearing date. They are not entitled to costs, but neither are they exposed to an order against them for costs. Costs may still be paid out of the estate, which may affect them indirectly.

This means that people who would otherwise be parties can opt out of the process. This is tempting for people who are risk-averse. Most people are highly suspicious of legal proceedings and want no part of them. This rule permits them to keep out. Because estate litigation usually involves "Other People's Money", some people do not want to share in the outcome of the case where that involves the effort of the contest and the risk of loss.

THE BATTLE LINES

As with all civil litigation, lawyers for the parties should be aware - acutely aware - of shared interests, potential alliances and conflicts. At the initial interview, the estate lawyer should ask who else could be a client on the same side, both to share the cost and to support the position.

Decision-makers should not take into account how many people take one position or another. However, as with the **_Jafari_** case cited below, judges have to be practical. If there is little evidence to support the continuation of litigation, they may well cut it short. Imagine a motions judge or master facing the lawyer who represents several siblings opposed to another who represents only one sibling. The appearance of justice favoring the many is itself an obstacle to be overcome by the one acting solo.

Jafari is instructive for another reason. Is there any money at stake? It is one thing to insist upon one's legal rights. It is quite another to insist upon legal rights where there is a substantial value that will change with the outcome. The courts have an overriding equitable principle, "_de minimis_ *non curat lex*" [the law does not concern itself with trivial matters]. In *Jafari*, the son was not entitled to a day in court in part because he never established that the estate value was worth the considerable effort involved in continued litigation.

Why does this matter?

As with any civil litigation, lawyers have to get the parties right. Unlike civil litigation, it may not be obvious who the "right" parties are. Consider these:

• Who will sign the retainer agreement?

• Who will cross-examine whom (should it come to that)?

• Who will be served with documents as the opposition?

• Who might sign a supporting affidavit?

• Who will be the audience for any particular presentation?

• Who will participate in the end-game (the settlement meeting or the contested application hearing)?

Case studies

KORSTEN V. LOVETT AND JAFARI V. ATTAR-JAFARI

Korsten v. Lovett 2002 CanLII 10598 (ON SC), http://canlii.ca/t/1cjwr

Jafari v. Attar-Jafari 2008 CanLII 37212 (ON SC), http://canlii.ca/t/1zt79

Consider the decision in *Jafari*:

> *[13] I find the Applicant ... merely made an assertion as to an interest and did not present sufficient evidence to establish a genuine interest in the estate. He presented to the court no medical opinion that his father was incompetent around the time the Will was prepared and executed. In the circumstances of this case, being an offspring of the testator by itself, I find, is not a sufficient basis to qualify as a person who appears to have a financial interest in the estate or from which to infer an interest might exist. There is no evidence to suggest there might be a previous Will or a subsequent Will or Codicil on which the Applicant might base his contention. Beyond the fact that the Applicant is a son of the testator, he presents little else to support his view.*

This case may have been decided differently had the son of the deceased presented more evidence to support his argument. One could argue that striking the will creates an intestacy which in turn creates an interest in favour of the son (to some extent) under the **Succession Law Reform Act**.

The outcome of this case shows the importance of case analysis and spin. Clearly, the judge felt that this was a trivial estate and that the applicant had little in support of the application. Consider the contrary outcome in *Korsten* where the possible intestacy was sufficient to create the financial interest intended by the rules. Interestingly, this decision was cited and distinguished in ***Jafari***. The only distinction that appears on the record is the absence of evidence from the applicant.

> *[8] In the book Probate Practice by MacDonnell, Sheard and Hull (4th), the authors write at page 21 as follows:*
>
>> *"The term 'financial interest' is not defined in the rules and presumably includes any interest in property that a person may have under the terms of any testamentary instrument duly executed by the deceased person, or on an intestacy of that deceased person, whether such interest is vested, vested subject to being divested, or contingent."*
>
> *[9] The only case that the parties were able to produce to the Court was the case of **Smith v. Vance**, 1997 Carswell Ont 1554. That is a decision of Justice Sills.*
>
> *[10] The facts of that case are that the deceased apparently had by a previous will, which was destroyed, made the Applicant a beneficiary. Under a subsequent will she had not made the Applicant a beneficiary.*
>
> *[11] The Applicant in that case questioned the testamentary capacity of the deceased person.*

*[12] Justice Sills in that case at Paragraph 10
wrote as follows:*

> *"However, claimants must do more than
> simply assert an interest. They must present
> sufficient evidence of a genuine interest and
> meet a threshold test to justify inclusion as a
> party. It need not be conclusive evidence at
> the stage but must be evidence capable of
> supporting an inference that the claim is one
> that should be heard."*

Justice Sills goes on at paragraph 11:

> *"If the evidence offered by an objector is
> capable of supporting an inference that the
> claim raises a genuine issue and thus is one
> that should be heard, the objector is entitled
> to standing and should be granted
> permission to be added as a party."*

> *...*

*[15] The will under review was executed on
February 6, 2002. It does not have as a beneficiary
the Applicant. If the will is not proven then the
Applicant would have a right to take on intestacy,
as she is one of the three granddaughters, unless a
previous will is located and if valid and she is not
made a beneficiary. I am advised that previous wills
had been destroyed at the direction of the deceased.*

CHAPTER 6: MANDATORY MEDIATION

- *Mediation is mandatory for a good reason.*

- *Mediation in estate litigation is different than in other forms of litigation.*

- *Tactics and decisions reflect the parties' "interests" more than their legal rights.*

WHY IS MEDIATION MANDATORY IN ESTATE LITIGATION?

The short answer is because Rule 75.1 makes it so. The order for directions "may" set out the mediation parameters. In Ottawa, Toronto and Windsor, the "applicant shall" bring a motion to seek direction for conduct of the mediation. Therefore, it makes sense for the order for directions under Rule 75 to cover the same ground as that required by 75.1.

Mediation works particularly well in estate cases. Parties confront each other in plenary session. They then consider their positions in caucus. An independent professional (the mediator) serves as referee and cheerleader for a peaceful solution. Often, the mediator gives opinions that influence how parties see their positions and those of the opposition.

While estate litigation does not require a specialist mediator, it is often helpful that the mediator be familiar with estate cases. One of the guiding principles for any mediation is that the parties consider the BATNA (the best alternative to a negotiated agreement). If they do not know what will come next after mediation fails, how can they assess that alternative?

Because of the emotions involved, mediators with an understanding of family law often work with estate cases. If they are not familiar with the operations of the estate rules, such mediators may become more dependent upon the lawyers for guidance as to what will happen next should the case not settle.

TACTICS IN ESTATE LITIGATION

There are separate, distinct events within mediation sessions. Consider these:

1. The first decision in respect of mediation is the selection of the mediator. Because estate litigation is different, it is often advisable for estate practitioners to serve as mediators. Alternately, professional mediators with - experience in estate cases are often preferable. The value of this will be evident as the mediator deals with individual clients, who often require special handling.

2. In most mediation, the parties agree to exchange briefs beforehand. A mediation brief usually puts forward the position of the party. In estate cases, however, counsel should be very careful about using inflammatory language such as adjectives and accusations. Not only do these decrease the likelihood of settlement, they may cause greater

animosity between the parties. There is animosity enough to go around in most estate cases. Lawyers should not add tinder to the fire.

3. Most mediation sessions take place at a lawyer's office or at the office of an independent institution, such as an examiner's office or the courthouse. Because of the emotions involved in many estate cases, lawyers should go out of their way to reduce the suspicion that the location of the mediation session somehow indicates a disadvantage to the client. The same is true with the selection of the mediator.

4. Estate cases usually involve parties who know each other, have a long history in common, and really don't want to be involved in a court fight. Each party thinks, "It's somebody else's fault." And often for reasons not germane to the actual dispute. Emotions run high. Suspicions are high. Tensions are high. Trust is low. Goodwill is nonexistent. Lawyers on all sides usually agree that a mediated settlement is preferable to continued litigation, even one that does not specifically favour their clients. They should form a team to do whatever it takes to reduce the stress and increase the conditions conducive to settlement. Often, this requires coordination among the lawyers and the mediator. Often, this coordination should start before the mediation session. What can the lawyers do to increase the chance of settlement, through discussion, through stipulation, or through

disclosure? This is an appropriate discussion throughout the case, but especially on the eve of mediation.

5. At the outset of the mediation session, it is common for the mediator to convene a plenary session where all the parties and lawyers meet in the same conference room. The mediator has a brief introduction and then turns to one of the lawyers and asks for an opening address. The lawyers make their addresses (sales pitches) that argue for the likely success of their cause. So much for the norm. In estate cases, this usually does not work well. Consider whether an opening address is appropriate at all. There is no rule that requires one. Alternately, consider using the opening address to deliver a message of goodwill. The lawyer's client wants to settle. The lawyer's client appreciates the honesty, integrity and sincerity of the other parties. The lawyer's client is prepared to compromise positions so as to accommodate competing needs and views. If this is reciprocated by the opposition, the chances for settlement increase dramatically.

6. Offer and counter-offer tactics in estate cases are different, as well. Dealing only with offers (including counteroffers), lawyers should wrap the offer in the softest possible language. The offer should express the interests (as opposed to the rights) of all parties. The lawyer may suggest that this offer represents a serious compromise of rights in order to reduce the stress of litigation. This offer

accounts for the position of the other parties. With that goal in mind, the lawyer may frame the terms of the offer to reconcile the competing positions of the parties rather than simply express what one party wants to accomplish.

7. The role of the mediator is different in estate cases. Just as with family law, the mediator is the "adult" in a room of bickering parties. The parties think that the lawyers for the opposition parties are really part of the problem, and not part of the solution. The mediator, on the other hand, may be seen as the voice of reason who can rescue the parties from their mutually destructive behavior. For this reason, it is common for mediators to meet with the clients separately, even without their lawyers. This is almost unheard of in civil litigation, but quite common in estate cases.

8. When mediation finishes, whether successfully or not, lawyers should do whatever they can to have the parties shake hands and acknowledge that they tried their best. These are usually people who have to deal with each other in the future. This is not a tort claim where an insurer and a plaintiff have no reason for further dealings. The mediator can make a gratuitous comment to the effect that the parties tried hard to resolve a very difficult situation. The lawyers should nod sagely. Again, the professionals in the room should do their level best to reduce stress, acknowledge the differences between the parties, and keep them talking to each other.

INTERESTS VS. LEGAL RIGHTS

Lawyers like to think that "it's all about the money". In estate cases, however, this is simply not true. The parties likely have a history with each other, and may have a future with each other as well. Sometimes parties simply want an acknowledgment of some apparent transgression or worthwhile sacrifice that took place in the past.

One would hope that no party has a legal interest in losing a lawsuit. In estate cases, however, lawyers hear far too often that parties are willing to fight for the "principle" or to teach a lesson to the other party. The lawyers for all parties should deliver the "facts of life" speech early and often. Litigation should not be about anything other than the cause of the dispute. Lawyers should show their clients that the court will only adjudicate matters that have a legal significance presented in the proper manner.

Even so, lawyers should be on the lookout for what "drives" their clients. What seems irrational may become quite explicable when the drivers are identified. It then becomes incumbent upon the lawyers to deal with the causes of the litigation, and not only the legal issue in dispute.

Returning to the subject of case analysis for a moment, lawyers should frame the issue in a manner that accommodates what really separates the parties. This may not be observable early in the case. At mediation, it should be apparent what drives all the parties. Unlike civil litigation, the drivers might be totally different from one party to the next. One party may be trying to teach the other one a lesson, whereas another party is in it for the money. One party may want to prevent misconduct later, where the other wants judicial recognition of righteous conduct.

During mediation, the drivers that motivate each of the parties may well prevent them from settling their case. It is often the first goal of the mediator to determine what the real causes are for the litigation. The mediator may rely upon the lawyers for input, but may determine that the lawyers are unreliable in this respect.

Why does this matter?

Mediation is well-suited for estate cases. Consider the combination of:

- emotional involvement,

- costs and uncertainty of litigation, and

- the likelihood that some or all the parties are dealing with other people's money.

These dictate that mediation should work. It actually does so far more often in estate cases than in civil litigation. Counsel should seize the opportunity (*carpe diem*) in the best interests of their clients. Fortunately, the Rules encourage exactly this.

Lawyers who settle cases at mediation will find that clients and other lawyers will refer cases to them. It is a case of win, win, win.

Case study: Re: Sheard Estate

2013 ONSC 7729 (CanLII), http://canlii.ca/t/g2cks

For obvious reasons, there is not much in the way of reported decisions concerning estate mediation. However, this is a case in which executors applied to pass their accounts. Some of the beneficiaries banded together to file a notice of objection that required a detailed set of accounts supported by vouchers (cheque stubs, receipts, invoices and the like). They were doing so as a step towards withdrawing an interim release they had given earlier. Such releases usually accompany interim distributions to the beneficiaries.

The case that involved mediation was that the beneficiaries asked the motions judge for an order to dispense with mandatory mediation. The judge had this to say about mandatory mediation:

> *[40] Any application to pass accounts is subject to the mandatory mediation provisions of the Rule 75.1. The grandchildren say the court should exercise its discretion under rule 75.1.04 and dispense with the necessity of mediation in this case. They seem to be suggesting that since their primary complaint is over executors' compensation, the quarrel is not really among family members, and thus is less amenable to mediation. I disagree. Mediation is helpful in narrowing issues, focusing cases, and, where possible settling them. Mediation is useful in every kind of litigation before our*

courts. Its efficacy is not limited to "family relationship" disputes.

Further reading

__Mediation for Civil Practitioners: issues and solutions__

CHAPTER 7: AFFIDAVITS IN ESTATE CASES

- *Most evidence is presented to the court in the form of affidavits.*

- *Affidavits identify the parties, present the facts, frame the issues, and propose solutions.*

- *In contested estate litigation, opposing parties have the right of cross-examination.*

PRESENTATION OF EVIDENCE

The Rules allow for pleadings in a more traditional format, such as Statement of Claim and Statement of Defence. Even so, most estate cases proceed by notice of application or motion within an application.

Except where all parties consent to the relief claimed, applications and motions consist of a record. The moving party's record will contain a notice of application (or motion) and the affidavit evidence in support. Respondents file a record with their affidavits and cross-motion (if any). The court therefore often has more than one record. This is similar to the practice in motions court in civil litigation. In civil trials, the trial record consists of all pleadings of the main parties.

As seen in the earlier chapter involving motions for directions, the applicant or moving party wants to accomplish something in the litigation. That is usually the relief claimed. Why is the applicant entitled to that relief? Those are the grounds, recited in summary fashion in the notice.

The grounds are simply positions taken until they are proved. The proof starts with an affidavit, in which someone with relevant knowledge asserts the facts to be true. The order for directions will identify who plays the role of plaintiff and defendant, if that is the procedure that the parties choose or that the court imposes. The order may provide directions as to who will provide evidence by way of affidavit as well as who will be cross-examined and by which other parties.

WHAT SHOULD BE SET OUT IN AN AFFIDAVIT?

Everything that the deponent knows that belongs in the grounds section of the motion or application should be set out in the affidavit of that deponent. However, the full contents should reflect the case analysis conducted by the lawyer preparing the affidavit.

- What is the issue?

- What are the elements that have to be established?

- What can this witness say to support those elements?

- What is the theory of the opponents?

- What can this witness say to attack that theory?

- Because of the right of cross-examination, counsel must also consider the risks: what can this witness say that will work against the position taken by the lawyer's client?

Each of these questions should be answered before virtual pen is set to virtual paper. In effect, the affidavit becomes a pleading with respect to the facts. Affidavits do not set out law, but they can and should set out all of the facts that give rise to the desired legal outcome.

WHAT TONE SHOULD AN AFFIDAVIT ADOPT?

Lawyers who prepare affidavits should bear in mind the likely audience. Obviously, it is intended that the judge see a record that includes this affidavit at some point. Not so obviously, the drafting lawyer wants the affidavit to have some impact on the opposition. In the case of estate litigation, it is not helpful to adopt as a default the tone of total aggression. Accusations often come back to haunt the accuser.

Estate litigation should involve a strategy to accomplish an effective settlement as early as possible. Therefore affidavits should not inflame with unsupported allegations or accusations. They should rarely "name drop", a strategy in which they allege that some other party or witness has knowledge which may or may not be true.

Because many of the causes of estate litigation involve suspected misconduct, it is common to allege a cover-up or a conspiracy. For example, three siblings might band together to keep a fourth sibling from participating in an estate. As another example, one sibling overlooks misconduct by a second so that the first might avoid scrutiny. It is said that undue influence does not occur in the light of day, but usually behind closed doors and in secrecy. Estate litigation often involves one party taking advantage of another party, either by misrepresentation, by failure of disclosure or by abuse of a trust.

The tone of the affidavits should reflect the bare facts. A tone of righteous indignation usually provokes a response with a similar tone. The judge will read all of the material to get to the facts, and will not appreciate that tone. Better for the party to state the facts in as flat a manner as possible. Adjectives and pejoratives can be saved for the examination, either in the examiner's office or at trial.

WHO SHOULD MAKE AN AFFIDAVIT?

It is expected that the parties to estate litigation will each submit an affidavit. Even if one party provides the details and another allied party simply agrees, it is usually best for all parties to present their positions in the form of an affidavit.

Strictly speaking, the rules of evidence are lifted somewhat. Rule 39.01(5) provides that

"An affidavit for use on an application may contain statements of the deponent's information and belief with respect to facts that are not contentious, if the source of the

information and the fact of the belief are specified in the affidavit."

This explains why affidavits often contain an introductory paragraph which states, "The deponent has personal knowledge of the facts set out in this affidavit, except where stated otherwise."

There is a practice where a lawyer will swear an affidavit on behalf of a client. Sometimes, a clerk in the office of the lawyer will swear the affidavit. Whenever it is anticipated that the motion will provoke contested proceedings, this is a bad practice for several reasons.[5]

- Lawyers who swear affidavits cannot appear as counsel of record on the motion or application where the affidavit is presented in evidence. They should not even sit at counsel table.

- Lawyers who swear affidavits waive solicitor-client privilege, to all or some extent. If they were not authorized to give that waiver, they may incur personal liability.

- Lawyers who swear affidavits can be cross-examined, and may not appreciate the significance of this.

- Lawyers who swear affidavits can be barred from further acting on the file. If the lawyer is likely to be a witness at a contested hearing, then the firm for which the lawyer is a partner or an employee may

---

[5] From the Ontario Rules of Professional Conduct.

also be barred from further acting on the file. The client may not be pleased with this result.

- Clerks make poor witnesses in contested proceedings. Usually, their evidence will be limited to what the lawyer told them. This is a poor alternative to avoid the lawyer being called to account. The client should swear the affidavit, if at all possible. Failing the client, some other witness should be found not directly related to the office of the lawyer.

THE SPECTRE OF CROSS-EXAMINATION

Lawyers should anticipate that their deponents may be cross-examined. This suggests three specific strategies that lawyers should keep in mind:

- First, lawyers should not file affidavits from witnesses who they want to keep away from the witness stand. Some deponents make poor witnesses, whose performance cannot be improved by preparation. Some deponents have knowledge that could harm the case. Some deponents have questionable loyalties and may spring a surprise during direct or cross-examination. Some deponents will actually work with the opposition. Opposing counsel may use the opportunity of cross-examination specifically to exploit some weakness that will harm the case for which the deponent's affidavit was submitted in the first place.

- Second, lawyers should consider "inoculation". This is a tactic discussed in the ***Examinations*** handbook in the YAS. The idea is that a few answers in direct might explain away some negative point to defuse the expected cross-examination on that very point later. The witness can deliver the explanation in the most favourable light.

- Third, and it bears repeating, affidavits should not provoke indignation on the part of the opposition. Even where the evidence is controversial and adversarial, it should be framed as neutrally as is consistent with establishing the elements that are required from case analysis.

Why does this matter?

No matter how skillful an advocate may be in public speaking and persuasion, the evidence presented will dictate the result in most cases. Skillful preparation of affidavits goes a long way to achieving the objectives of estate litigation. Often, cases settle based on the presentation of the affidavits.

Case studies: Re Portrusching Estate and Chernetz v. Eagle Copters Ltd.

Portrusching Estate 2009 NSSC 229 (CanLII), http://canlii.ca/t/24xrp

This Nova Scotia case illustrates a common problem in any estate solicitor's office. A testator dies. The will cannot be found. A lawyer comes forward who prepared the will and attended to its execution. A copy of that will is presented to the court. The beneficiaries explain all of the circumstances, including the family relationships. Everyone who might be interested in the estate comes forward to explain their respective position. Should the court presume that the will is lost and therefore destroyed?

As an exercise, students should pretend that there is another relative who has something to say about whether the testator destroyed the will. Perhaps the estranged spouse is not so estranged after all? Perhaps there was an adopted child who everybody else hates, but who claims to have reconciled with the testator, causing the destruction of the will? Prepare an affidavit by which that relative contests the adoption of the lost will. Keep in mind the burden of proof and the necessary elements to support or oppose the presumption of destruction (*animus revocandi*).

Chernetz v. Eagle Copters Ltd. 2002 ABQB 986 (CanLII), http://canlii.ca/t/5gcd

This Alberta case did not involve an estate. It did, however, discuss the perils of having a lawyer swear an affidavit for use in a proceeding. The Alberta Rule 314[6] provided:

A person who has made an affidavit ... filed in any ... proceedings may be cross-examined on the affidavit without order.

---

[6] Ontario Rule 39.02 provides that "a party to a motion or application may cross examine the deponent of any affidavit served by a party who is adverse in interest on the motion or application."

In a motion to compel certain parties to produce records over which they claimed privilege, the lawyer for the plaintiffs swore an affidavit. When the parties tried to cross-examine the lawyer, the plaintiffs argued that they erred in filing the lawyer's affidavit. They sought to tender new affidavits from three of the plaintiffs in place of the lawyer's affidavit (which they should have done in the first place). The defendants conceded that they would not ask that the lawyer be precluded from acting further as counsel in the case, but they insisted upon the cross-examination. The Court supported the motion and compelled the cross-examination.

The decision illustrates that the ability of the lawyer to continue to represent his clients was placed in jeopardy by the "mistake".

CHAPTER 8: DISCOVERY AND CROSS-EXAMINATIONS ON AFFIDAVITS

- *Estate examinations are similar, in theory, to pretrial examinations in civil litigation.*

- *Because of family relationships, tone and tactics should reflect the specific requirements of the case.*

- *The right to cross does not mean the questions must be cross.*

- *Use of the transcript is different in motions court than at trial.*

- *The purpose for the affidavit may change, but the answers given in the transcript apply throughout.*

WHAT IS THE PROCESS?

The decision to use pleadings instead of affidavits changes the name of the examination from cross-examination to discovery. Little else changes. The scope of the examination is broad enough to include all of the issues under consideration. Counsel is not restricted to the "four corners of the affidavit". Any matter in issue that is within the knowledge of the witness is fair game for the examination. Questions are not improper only because they are framed as cross-examination.

The order for directions should establish all of the procedural aspects of the examinations, including:

- Who will be examined, by whom and, if necessary, where.

- What restrictions or requirements should apply to the examination, including the time allowed for it.

- What documentary productions are required, by whom and when.

CROSS-EXAMINATION

Just because the lawyer has the right to cross-examine a witness does not mean that the tenor of the examination must be adversarial. Just like in civil litigation, examinations can take the form of an inquiry into the unknown, a follow-up of leads and a cross examination on points of vulnerability.

Unlike civil litigation, the relationship between the witness on the one hand and the other parties (including the client of the lawyer) may suggest that a softer touch is better. Lawyers can still ask the hard questions, but may consider doing so in a more gentle manner. Statements with questions can appear to be much less offensive than an outright cross-examination. For example, the witness says in an affidavit that the purpose of opening an account jointly with the testator was not only for the convenience of the testator. Cross-examination may look like this:

Q. I will now ask you questions about the opening of the joint account with the testator. You attended at the bank on October 3, correct?

A. Yes.

Q. With the testator, correct?

A. Yes.

Q. To open a chequing account, correct?

A. Yes.

Q. But all of the money was to come from the testator, correct?

A. Yes, that was not the intention at that time.

Q. But that's what occurred, correct?

A. Yes.

The witness will clearly feel that the lawyer is exerting a loss of control. This feels like a stressful examination. Certainly, this is no fun for the witness. Now consider an alternative method:

Q. You have said in your affidavit that you attended at the bank to open a joint account with the testator. Please tell me about it.

Whatever information comes from the witness, counsel can still ask follow-up questions. It may be that the information received covers all of the same ground. It also may open up other areas for inquiry. The examiner remains free to attack, should the situation warrant.

Both methods are available to the cross-examiner. It is suggested here that the examiner consider both, rather than only the first of the methods.

NON-PARTY WITNESSES

In the case of non-parties, the interests of those witnesses must be accommodated. The Rules in respect of civil cases deal with the role of non-parties, both with respect to attendance for examination and production of documents.[7] The order for directions, on the other hand, has to provide for any applicable process in respect of non-parties.

Non-party witnesses are common in estate litigation. Consider these common actors:

- The lawyer who drafted the will or power of attorney.

- The medical service providers.

- The capacity assessor.

- Staff of financial institutions.

- Outside professionals (such as realtor, financial advisor, insurance agent).

---

[7] Rules 31.10 (discovery) and 30.10 (documents).

They may all have eyewitness and documentary evidence to provide. Each must be handled with respect and deference. Lawyers should schedule the examination to accommodate such witnesses and their agendas. Preparation sessions should be tailored with the goal of preparation and not of coaching. "Conduct money" should also be considered.

Is what the non-party witness has to say controversial? Is it necessarily adversarial, and against whom?

USE OF THE TRANSCRIPT

Where a trial is unlikely, contested proceedings occur by presentation of records, transcripts and oral argument. Judges and Masters do not want to read any part of the transcript that is not highlighted by counsel. For that reason, counsel should refer to specific portions of the transcript in their briefs. It is customary to attach copies of the relevant portions as tabs in the brief submitted in advance.

This has significance to the examination itself. First, a witness should be directed to the relevant subject. This suggests use of a "headline" that introduces the subject in a manner that is relevant to the questions that follow. It also suggests that all questions about the subject occur one after the other. It becomes confusing to attach the page from one part of the transcript to another page from another part which may cover the same subject. This invites opposing counsel to identify still other parts of the transcript that deal with the same subject. The result is highly confusing to anyone who tries to piece the information together.

As noted earlier, affidavits may deal with information, knowledge and belief provided that the source is identified. Cross-examinations may elicit hearsay evidence. There is no jury involved into the decision-making. The Judge or Master can apply the appropriate weight to whatever evidence appears to be offside the rules of evidence.

TRANSCRIPTS ARE NOT SINGLE USE DOCUMENTS

Lawyers should be careful when they tender a witness to be examined or when they conduct an examination of an opposition witness. There are circumstances in which words spoken by the witness can come back to haunt.

Where the witness testifies to support some procedural step early in the litigation, those words may be useful for a contrary purpose at a procedural step that occurs later in the proceedings. Worse, those words can be the subject of an impeachment during a later cross-examination should the witness try to back away from them. Consider, for example, the case where the witness deposes in an affidavit that there are no assets in an estate, whether of a grantor of a power of attorney or of the deceased person. In both cases, this allegation may be helpful to avoid the appointment of a trustee, accountant or other intervening professional. Later, however, these words will be harmful in a claim for security for costs because the estate is insolvent. They may cause the attorney or estate trustee to be made personally liable for some subsequent step.

In other words, lawyers should always look at the Big Picture. This is one of the reasons why the affidavit in support of a motion for directions should be as neutral as possible. Who can foretell exactly what position the deponent will take in later circumstances? Best to keep options open.

Transcripts have many uses now. They are recited during mediation, pretrial sessions, motions and are read into the record at trial as part of the case of one adverse party or another. Lawyers should be careful what they ask, because the words of the witness can be used for many of these purposes and for any party.

Witnesses may become incapable of testifying for health reasons or because they leave the jurisdiction for a sustained time. Consider that estate cases often involve ill or elderly people, either as the subject of the case or as a party or witness. Judges can allow the transcript in place of the testimony of the witness who cannot attend.

In each of these circumstances, if a lawyer gets an answer that hurts the case, that answer may stand up at trial without the opportunity for cross-examination. This suggests that the lawyer should use the opportunity as soon as it arises. It is rare indeed for lawyers to withhold their killer questions until trial. The stronger the position, the sooner it should be expressed. That runs counter to the way lawyers were trained decades ago. It is the modern way, however.

Why does this matter?

As with all out-of-court examinations, there are several purposes for each discovery or cross-examination. These are:

- Learn what the witness has to say.

- Try out the theory of the case to see whether the evidence supports the theory.

- Challenge the position of the witness, and of the opposing party (if different).

- Persuade the opposition to take your own position more seriously and to doubt the efficacy of their position.

Overall, the purpose is to position the case to settle favorably. The examination is just one tool to accomplish that. Counsel should keep in mind this objective and make sure that the examination does not make its accomplishment more difficult.

Case study: Re Hammond Estate

1999 CanLII 19754 (NL SCTD), http://canlii.ca/t/fww42

This Newfoundland case involved an old man with several nephews and nieces. When he became ill and hospitalized, one nephew acted on the power of attorney granted a few years previously. In hospital, the other relatives determined that the attorney was acting improperly because the old man was sickly and thin (and clearly not well looked after). Further, they allege that the attorney was selling the old man's house, which would be of no benefit to the old man. They brought a petition for appointment of a guardian and the ouster of the attorney.

The decision is instructive for several reasons.

- First, it is distressingly common. The Judge quoted a textbook from Gerald Roberts, ***Mental Disability and the Law in Canada (2nd Ed.)*** where he wrote that "Chronic and degenerative illness affecting mental capacity is becoming increasingly common. It is estimated that at least 10% of Canadians over the age of 65, and 20% of those over the age of 80 suffered from dementia of some kind." This explained the necessity for continuing powers of attorney by which the aging people could determine who would manage their affairs upon disability. For reasons similar to those in the ***Hammond*** case, this type of litigation occurs frequently across the country.

- Second, the judge ruled that there was a heavy onus on the part of the opposing relatives to prove that the attorney selected by the grantor was acting improperly. In this case, the old man was an eccentric. His weight and demeanor were his own choice. The lawyer who prepared the power of attorney testified that the old man had capacity and denied any influence from the appointed attorney, even though that attorney had brought him to the lawyer's office. Finally, the judge ruled that there was no evidence that the attorney was self-dealing.

Property ownership was examined and explained. No change was pending and so there was nothing to show self-dealing.

- Third, and quite significant in the modern day, is that the litigation was "caused" by the opposing relatives. The one who came forward was made to pay the legal costs of the attorney who prevailed. In some cases, costs are paid out of the estate of the grantor or testator. More commonly these days, the court will look for the party who caused litigation and saddle that party with the costs.

As an exercise, accept the facts alleged by the opposing relatives. Craft an argument, based upon case analysis, that the attorney should be replaced. Then, consider a negligence claim against the solicitor who prepared the power of attorney. Assuming that the court ruled in favor of the opposing relatives to set aside that power of attorney, create an argument that the solicitor should pay the damages for premature conveyance of real estate and for costs of the litigation to set aside the power of attorney.

Further reading

Discovery Techniques: a practical guide to the discovery process in civil actions

CHAPTER 9: PROVING YOUR CASE AT TRIAL: DIRECT EXAMINATIONS

- *Case analysis should inform every series of questions asked during direct examinations.*

- *Direct examinations are the viva voce versions of affidavits tendered by witnesses in favor of the party.*

- *The back story often becomes more important than in civil litigation.*

- *Consider what is relevant. Avoid expressions of ill will.*

CASE ANALYSIS

What is the issue? Once framed, what does the lawyer have to prove or disprove to succeed on that issue? This analysis should dictate what is important and what is not. On both sides of the issue.

The analysis that spins the case for the lawyer's client will be the focus of the direct examination. This includes both the facts and the spin on those facts. The analysis of the opposition's case will inform the direct examiner how best to inoculate the witness. Inoculation is testimony that the lawyer draws from the witness during direct examination that pre-empts effective cross-examination by opposing counsel.

This does not exclude evidence pertaining to the back story (see below), but it does inform what part of the back story is important.

CONTINUATION OF AFFIDAVITS

The motion for directions (if any) may have dictated the submission of pleadings. The parties may rely upon the affidavits in the application and responding records. The difference, of course, is that the affidavit is sworn and the statement of claim/defence is a position paper.

Parties can be cross-examined on their pleadings. However, the easy escape is to say that that was a position based upon facts known or believed at the time. This is not possible with affidavits. Where statements are sworn and later disproved, the deponent may be hard-pressed to escape effective impeachment.

Because estate cases usually involve families and lengthy history, lawyers must keep the witness on message. The less time the witness testifies, the easier this becomes. The obverse is also true: the longer the witness testifies in chief, the greater the opportunity for a successful cross-examination on some overreaching or misstatement.

Typically, a party-witness will have produced an affidavit prior to the hearing of the case. Hopefully, that affidavit was set out as neutrally as possible. By the time of the hearing, however, the gloves are off. Positions of all parties are known. Alliances are fixed in place. Now, the objective is to persuade the decision-maker more so than the opposition. As lawyers direct their witnesses, they want to hear the spin (adjectives, adverbs, evocative language) that makes their case. For example, if the lawyer wants to establish that the opposing party failed to live up to some standard or to comply with some duty, the lawyer wants to hear the word "abandon" or some such word to underline the significance of this failure.

Indeed, this illustrates the necessity for case analysis. The favorable iteration will contain each of the elements as spun to provide the best result possible to persuade the decision-maker. This becomes the task of counsel, to get the witness to provide the raw material for the persuasion. Without this, the lawyer is restricted during submissions for making that killer argument.

BACK STORY

Estate cases are rife with back story. Each witness has a different perspective as to who did what to whom and when. It is the job of the lawyer to distinguish relevant from irrelevant. The outline for the direct examination should identify what the lawyer needs by way of back story. It is up to the lawyer to weave this into the examination.

Preparation of the witness should include both the basic elements and the appropriate back story. The lawyer should make the witness familiar with the order in which these topics will be raised. Why is this testimony relevant to what the witness has to say? In some circumstances, within the discretion of the lawyer, the witness should be made to understand how this fits into the dispute. Such witnesses will be better prepared to fill in the blanks where the direct questions are less than perfect. It will also help them withstand cross-examination.

"Mom always liked you best". Unfortunately, this allegation often forms the basis of the litigation that lawyers face today. This is no joke. The testator may have given a major asset to a child in recognition of a close relationship. The testator may have chosen one sibling over another as executor or attorney. These choices reflect both recognition of skills and a level of trust. How easy is it for the other relatives to misinterpret the choice as being an irrational preference based upon undue influence.

ACCUSATIONS VS. PETTY ILL WILL

This is equally true in family law cases and in commercial cases where the parties know each other well. The court does not want to hear all of the "dirty laundry". The court does want to hear anything that weighs on the issues to be decided and the credibility of the respective parties.

In estate cases, there is often an issue arising out of "trust" or "fiduciary duty". This involves trust by beneficiaries or other stakeholders in the good faith of the attorney, guardian, trustee or advisor. If there are facts that raise the suspicion of the court that there was an abuse of that trust, those facts are important. If on the other hand, the witness is simply "slinging mud" about someone else, the court will use that accusation as a reason for dismissing the testimony of the witness as being partisan, dramatic or otherwise untrustworthy.

There may be a fine line drawn between accusation and ill will. It is up to the lawyer to draw that distinction. It is up to the witness to deliver the lines in a way that favors the former conclusion. It is up to the cross-examiner to ask the questions that favor the latter conclusion. Indeed, this may form a substantial part of the basis for a cross-examination. During the direct examination, the lawyer who called the witness should inoculate against that very cross.

Why does this matter?

Direct examinations are no walk in the park. They are an application of case analysis. Properly handled, a direct examination will advance the case of the lawyer and harm the case of the opposition. Counsel should be mindful that the reverse is possible. By allowing for what can go wrong, counsel can minimize the risks and maximize the benefits.

Case study: Russell v. Fraser

1980 CanLII 737 (BC CA), http://canlii.ca/t/24cdn

This British Columbia case involves what is fortunately an uncommon situation. The deceased was an old woman who was a customer of a local credit union. She was distant from her nephews and nieces. She retained a solicitor recommended by the credit union manager, Fraser, for the purpose of drawing up her will. This retainer failed over confusion as to whether the estate was greater than the identified legacies. Later, the deceased directed the manager himself to prepare the will for her. This is the uncommon situation.

The manager suggested that he be named as the executor and as residuary beneficiary. He gave those instructions to a junior lawyer in the same office of the other lawyer. The junior lawyer did as he was told, attended on the client (in the absence of the manager). There was an issue involving the drafting of the residuary clause. If Fraser predeceased the testator, what then? In direct examinations, Fraser's testimony was uncertain as was that of the junior solicitor. Ultimately, the court upheld the will but struck out the residuary clause.

The decision is instructive for several reasons:

- First, it is an excellent recitation of the law with respect to "suspicious circumstances" as it then applied.

- Second, it analyzes the difference in the testimony between the two principal witnesses on the subject that bothered the court, the residuary clause and instructions given.

- Third, the costs ruling demonstrates the importance of establishing who "caused" the litigation. Because the trial judge chose not to blame Fraser, costs of the trial were paid out of the estate. Clearly, however, Fraser caused the appeal, and therefore he had to pay those costs. Reflecting the old practice, Fraser's costs of the trial were paid out of the estate. It is unlikely that this would be the case today.

- Generally speaking, estate litigation is a fact-oriented. As repeated by Justice Robert Beaudoin of the Ontario Superior Court, there are very few "lawsuits" and a great many "fact suits". Although the law of suspicious circumstances dictated the analysis of the court, the direct examinations of the two principal witnesses determined the outcome far more than did the law.

As an exercise, think of all the suspicious circumstances that might dictate that a testator did not either understand or freely execute a will. The decision refers to several of these. Students should list each of the ones referred to by the trial judge. However, this list is not even close to exhaustive. Students should make up facts and suggest other circumstances that might pertain that would raise the suspicions of the court enough to warrant a reverse of the onus of proof.

Further reading

Examinations in Civil Trials: the formula for success

Outlining: how to structure examinations in civil litigation

Vout v. Hay, [1995] 2 SCR 876, 1995 CanLII 105 (SCC), http://canlii.ca/t/1frj3 (on suspicious circumstances)

CHAPTER 10: PROVING YOUR CASE AT TRIAL: CROSS-EXAMINATIONS

- *Case analysis focuses the attention on what has to be proved/disproved.*

- *Cross-examinations should be short, and targeted.*

- *Bad answers should be impeachable.*

- *Cross can do more harm than good.*

- *Cross examiners should not participate in the ill will that may arise between the parties. Cool, calm demeanor will win the day.*

CASE ANALYSIS

At the risk of over-repetition, case analysis should inform every outline section and every series of question asked. The decision-maker will be attentive to protect family members from attack. Counsel should be careful to avoid ill will and petty attacks on irrelevant or trivial misconduct.

The key word is "irrelevant". Case analysis establishes what is relevant and what is not. Back story elements should be avoided in cross-examination unless the point is to attack credibility.

Because many of the elements will be remote from current day affairs, cross-examiners may spend more time to establish lack of memory than outright deceit. Courts prefer to find the former than the latter. This is less true with witnesses or parties who are not part of the family history, such as professional advisors or institutional service providers.

SHORT AND TO THE POINT

A default preparation for cross-examination might well occur this way:

- What is the issue to which this witness can contribute?

- What are the elements that go into making this issue a winner?

- Identify each of the facts that go into each necessary element. How many of these are controversial?

- Focus on the controversial facts. Give each one a separate heading in the outline.

- For each heading, use the five-and-out method presented in the ***Discovery Techniques*** and ***Examinations*** handbooks. Make the point as quickly as possible. Leave the conclusion unstated, but implied (where possible).

- Where possible, leave room for a section in the outline on credibility. Attacks on credibility can come from:

  o lack of memory,

o medical issues,

o outright bias, and

o previous inconsistent statements.

Typically, cross-examiners have a lot of raw material upon which to base a cross-examination. There are the parties themselves who arm their lawyers with lots of information, both relevant and not. There are the transcripts of examinations conducted during the litigation. There are written records of transactions, both from the parties and from outside sources, such as real estate records, bank records, medical clinical notes and records, and the like.

Much of the cross-examination will consist of building up one witness as having better credibility or opportunity to observe or independence than another witness. One witness can testify about the credibility of another. For this reason, lawyers should pay attention to the motivation of the various parties and witnesses. Just because one party has called the witness to testify does not mean that this witness is fond of everybody testifying on behalf of that party. Typically, a witness in estate litigation knows a lot more than has been declared in the direct examination. The cross-examiner can use this, provided there is adequate preparation.

WHAT CAN GO WRONG?

Of course, all cross-examinations can lead to disaster. Here are several examples of how things can go wrong during estate litigation.

- The "question too many" can trigger an answer that causes some harm. The follow-up questions only make it worse. Counsel should be attentive to cut their losses when a sequence of questions does not proceed as hoped.

- Witnesses may change their tune, if not their outright testimony. Lawyers should have backup information upon which to base an impeachment. If they are not ready for this, they will lose all their own momentum as they fumble around looking for relevant documents or transcript excerpts.

- The cross-examiner starts to argue with the witness. Emotions can run high. Witnesses tend to give longer, detailed answers to questions that seek a simple "yes" response. Therefore, lawyers should be careful to phrase all of their questions as leading, to seek the answer "yes". If a different answer comes out, this will be a signal for the lawyer to pay special attention to the next questions. Even a simple "no" should provoke the lawyer to consider impeachment on the testimony just given or abandonment of a section of questions.

- Long answers should suggest that the witness has become an "advocate" for the party. They should use the opportunity of a long answer to pick out specific segments upon which to cross-examine further. They should resist the temptation to ask a long question or to sum up the long answer.

- The give-and-take of a cross-examination can appear to the decision-maker as overbearing, impolite or even brutal. Lawyers should keep their cool and continue with leading questions that solicit simple "yes" answers. They should moderate their tone (within their ability to do so). They should appear throughout to be reasonable searchers for the truth. All the lawyers in the courtroom know what the cross-examiner is trying to accomplish. Even so, the lawyer's calm demeanor will reduce the chance that the decision-maker over-corrects and sides with the witness.

IMPEACHMENT

At this point, students should revisit chapters on impeachment from their trial advocacy course. Impeachment is a ritual, complete with its formula. Failure to comply with the formula will lead to a loss of the opportunity for a dramatic success. Worse, the trial judge may hold it against the lawyer who tries and fails.

During the cross-examination, each point that the lawyer wants to make should be founded by some solid evidence elsewhere in the case. This may be testimony from other witnesses, testimony by this witness during the hearing or during a discovery, documentary evidence or evidence that will be adduced by another witness later in the case.

If the witness tries to wriggle out of a previous answer, the cross examiner should have the impeachment raw material available immediately. This allows the appearance of a relentless momentum that can crush the spirit of the witness. This can be very effective as a tool of persuasion.

This is not the time to explain how to perform impeachment. A three-minute refresher podcast is available at www.advocacyclub.ca/podcasts.

ILL WILL IN THE ADVERSARIAL PROCESS

As suggested earlier in this handbook, there is enough raw emotion and ill will in an estate case without the lawyer fanning the flames. Lawyers therefore must keep their cool and appear to be calm and rational throughout the case. This is particularly important in cross-examination.

One tactic may be to goad the witness into a demonstration of petty ill will. This may require fine-tuning, as not all witnesses will rise to the bait. The longer a cross-examination lasts, however, the less a witness can resist taking a shot at the opposing party or another witness. Lawyers should be careful when they provoke this, as it can backfire. Lawyers should only use neutral language unless they are quoting the witness directly.

Above all, the decision-maker should view the lawyer as independent from the animosity. Part of this can be established simply by professionalism in the courtroom. Consider these elements of professionalism:

- The absence of harsh words in the pleadings and affidavits.

- Polite and friendly relations between counsel.

- The obvious cooperation of counsel in preparation of joint exhibit books.

- The absence of silly or tactical objections.

- Concession of obvious points, with focus on the controversial ones.

Why does this matter?

Students consider cross-examination to be the pinnacle of the litigation process. It tends to be the scene of most of the high drama that occurs during a trial. However, cross-examination is simply one of the tools that lawyers have to advance their case and hinder that of the opposition. In estate cases, lawyers should be mindful that there are different pitfalls than in other civil litigation. By taking the interests of others into account, lawyers can improve their chance of success and minimize the negative fallout.

Case study: Graham v. Ellard

2011 BCSC 672 (CanLII), http://canlii.ca/t/flkl8

Mr. Graham died, leaving behind children and an ex-wife to whom he owed ongoing child support. The divorce decision left him a tenant in common of the family home, occupied by his ex-wife who had custody of the children. The home increased in value over time. The parties did not divide their pensions. The husband fell into arrears of support. The ex-wife became entitled to survivor benefits of the husband's pension on his death. This litigation involved the estate seeking part of the increase in value of the real estate and payment of occupation rent by the ex-wife. The ex-wife countered by claiming that she had caused the increase in value with her ongoing payments of mortgage and taxes and general upkeep. She argued that rewarding the estate was unjust enrichment.

This decision is instructive for a handbook of this nature because it breaks each of the claims for relief into its component analysis. Each element of the analysis has several factual elements that had to be proved. In one case, occupation rent, the trial judge noted the "forceful cross-examination" about when the youngest child ceased to be a "child of the marriage" as defined. However, each of the elements of each of the claims had to be proved and challenged.

As an exercise, students should consider each of the claims for relief separately. What evidence is required to make it out? How can that evidence be challenged? Students should create an outline of a cross-examination for the elements that are controversial.

This decision involves a case that recurs often in estate litigation. The thoughtful analysis of the trial judge is helpful to junior lawyers as they consider how to analyze the several issues that may occupy an estate litigation case.

Further reading

Examinations in Civil Trials: the formula for success

The Civil Courtroom: professionalism to build rapport

CHAPTER 11: CLOSING ARGUMENT AT TRIAL

- *Case analysis, but with all the evidence.*

- *Storytelling plays an important role.*

- *Techniques of persuasion are similar to those used in other litigation.*

- *Continuation of the contest for the More Reasonable Position.*

- *Must win vs. should win vs. accommodate all interests.*

CASE ANALYSIS

At each stage of the case, counsel prepare case analysis for preparation of the next step. This applies to motions, examinations, affidavits, briefs, everything. Even reporting letters. For closing arguments, however, there is one major difference. Everything is known that should be known. If it has not been led into evidence, it does not count.

Before the case began, counsel had some idea about what tactics to use to accomplish the best spin. What points should be highlighted? Which ones should be conceded? Which ones should be finessed, in the hopes that they would somehow disappear? At the end of the case, however, all of these tactics have been employed. Counsel for both sides know what the decision-maker heard. Also, counsel likely know the attitude of the decision-maker towards that evidence. Few judges avoid giving some indication of how they are thinking.

Case analysis acts like an outline for the argument. Add an introduction and a conclusion, and the elements will guide the lawyer through the speech. Judges often say that they would appreciate counsel writing the judgment for them during the argument. From the perspective of the judge, that may make sense. From the perspective of counsel, that request does not work. What assumptions must the lawyer make to arrive at the logical sequence? There are far too many, without guidance from the decision-maker.

Some judges are interactive during submissions. They ask questions. They make points. They express agreement or otherwise with particular points. Lawyers should cherish this interaction. Their case analysis should be flexible enough to permit them to change their presentation based upon how the decision-maker appears to react.

There is one technique that students should keep in mind for closing argument. If the judge asks a question, counsel must deal with it immediately. This may require that the lawyer juggle the balance of the submissions. If the judge expresses a thought pattern, that should become the focus of the lawyer. Plain and simple. Submissions are not made in the abstract. They are made to persuade. The judge, through the question, has invited the lawyer to persuade the judge on that point. That is an opportunity that should never be passed up. Right then and there. Deal with it.

CLOSING ARGUMENTS AS STORYTELLING EXERCISES

Estate cases involve family history. This can be the very stuff of a good story. Closing argument should rely upon that story, using the evidence to support the storytelling exercise. Unlike commercial litigation, estate litigation usually requires that the decision-maker pronounce upon the intention of parties at a remote time. This requires inference based upon circumstantial evidence. Often, that circumstantial evidence is wanting. Lawyers should use the gaps to support their version of the story, even with rhetorical questions and negative inferences.

Junior lawyers should not be become obsessed with the technical aspects of litigation, law and issue analysis. Estate litigation is simply an exercise in storytelling. In order to get to the punchline, however, a great deal of evidence must be introduced. Case analysis rejects the irrelevant and the trivial, spins the controversial and wraps it up with a bow. That, ultimately, is the closing argument.

Senior lawyers preach that they think of the final arguments as they are conducting the initial interview. That is only slightly true. In fact, senior lawyers consider how the events should be portrayed and how the facts will play out. Will this position "sell" to a judge? Based upon the answer to this, the interviewing lawyer asks the hard questions. These are the questions that the witness has to answer to succeed. That is quite different than crafting the actual argument. That said, each step of the litigation should advance the position that the lawyer wants to take at trial. In this respect, it will feed the final argument.

Storytelling has to accommodate what the law has to say about specific issues. Usually, however, lawyers will agree on what the law has to say. Adapting the perception of the facts (i.e. the evidence) to meet the law becomes the basis for closing argument. Storytelling is really the adaptation of the perception of the facts as presented during the trial.

When lawyers discuss the behavior of parties, they have to deal with facts that may portray the parties in a poor light. A lawyer who throws around accusations may trigger a negative response from the decision-maker. After all, the decision-maker knows people just like the ones under scrutiny. Lawyers should keep this in mind, namely that judges are people with relationships and experiences. The closing argument should accommodate what people such as the judge are likely to think about the events portrayed in the courtroom.

TECHNIQUES OF ESTATE STORYTELLING

Storytelling, to be effective, should adopt these techniques:

- The story has to be logical, even when the behavior of the parties was not.

- The story has to be compelling.

- The storyteller should be polite, calm, rational and merciful.

- The presentation should be as short and succinct as possible.

- The presenter should deal with the position of the opposition to have that position accommodated as much as possible.

- Specifically in estate litigation, storytelling should identify and work with the human elements of the parties.

THEME AND THEORY AND THE DECISION

When creating the story, the presenter should keep in mind the possibility that the judge will look for some common ground or accommodation. Because estate litigation involves "Other People's Money", judges often try to avoid punishing a party for minor misconduct. Costs can be paid out of the estate, even where one party is mainly responsible for causing the litigation. The decision-maker often has to balance the competing interests of innocent parties, as in the case of the surviving spouse having to compensate an ex-spouse for matters that arose in a prior marriage. Another example is where the claim of the named beneficiaries is at odds with the claim of a dependant who was inadequately covered by the will. What is fair may have nothing to do with what the law provides.

This gets back to the principle that estate litigation involves the Superior Court in its equitable jurisdiction far more than its interpretation of black letter law.

Consider then the theme and the theory of the case. The theory presents the elements that the party has to prove to succeed, to accomplish a legally correct result. The theme presents the spin that suggests why the parties should succeed, to accomplish a just result. Judges want to do what is fair. Especially in estate cases, where authority is very broad and legislation encourages equitable results, lawyers should press the "reasonable" and the "just" buttons. This often means that lawyers should express their claim for relief in a way that accommodates the opposition. In their own offices, lawyers may be thinking only about their clients. In court, they should consider the interests of the opposition with respect and expect the court to do the same.

WHO IS THE MOST REASONABLE PARTY?

Because of the equitable jurisdiction, courts frequently reward good behavior and punish bad behavior. It is therefore incumbent upon the lawyer to portray the client as having behaved as well as possible in these (difficult?) circumstances. The other party, however, failed to live up to proper social standards.

Throughout the case, each of the lawyers tries to portray the respective clients in the best or poorest light possible. The reason was to feed into the closing argument that the client of that lawyer behaved better than did the other.

The competition is partly a matter of which party performed better, a relative judgment, and partly a matter of who performed well, an absolute one. In a case where everybody performs adequately, the court may reward the party who performed well. Where all performed poorly, however, the court may be looking for who performed the best out of a bad lot of performers. Like the two hunters being chased by a bear, the one hunter may only have to outrun the other, and not try to outrun the bear.

Why does this matter?

Actually, it may not matter at all. Cases rarely get to trial. Cases that do get there rarely finish, because they are often settled before the last scheduled witness testifies. Judges usually form their own impressions and conclusions during the trial. They may not be influenced by closing argument, at least not much.

This is why lawyers rarely hold back their most important points to be used in closing argument. They use these points during discovery, cross-examination, motions, pretrials and throughout the trial. What good is a killer point if it is never used?

RULE 75 ESTATES: CONTENTIOUS PROCEEDINGS

Formal proof of testamentary instrument

75.01 An estate trustee or any person appearing to have a financial interest in an estate may make an application under rule 75.06 to have a testamentary instrument that is being put forward as the last will of the deceased proved in such manner as the court directs.

Proof of lost or destroyed will

75.02 The validity and contents of a will that has been lost or destroyed may be proved on an application,

(a) by affidavit evidence without appearance, where all persons who have a financial interest in the estate consent to the proof; or

(b) in the manner provided by the court in an order giving directions made under rule 75.06.

Objection to issuing certificate of appointment

Notice of Objection

75.03 (1) At any time before a certificate of appointment of estate trustee has been issued, any person who appears to have a financial interest in the estate may give notice of an objection by filing with the registrar or the Estate Registrar for Ontario a notice of objection (Form 75.1), signed by the person or the person's lawyer, stating the nature of the interest and of the objection.

Expiry, Withdrawal and Removal of Notice of Objection

(2) A notice of objection expires three years after it is filed and may be withdrawn by the person who filed it at any time before a hearing for directions under rule 75.06 in an application for the certificate or may be removed by order of the court. O. Reg. 484/94, s. 12.

Notice to Applicant

(3) Where an application for a certificate of appointment of estate trustee has been made and a notice of objection is filed, the registrar shall send notice of the filing (Form 75.2) by regular letter mail to the applicant or the applicant's lawyer at the mailing address shown in the application.

Notice to Objector

(4) An applicant who receives a notice under subrule (3) shall serve on the objector a notice to objector (Form 75.3) and file a copy of the notice and proof of service with the court.

(5) Where the objector does not serve and file a notice of appearance (Form 75.4) within 20 days after service of the notice to objector, the application shall proceed as if the notice of objection had not been filed.

Motion for Directions

(6) If the applicant does not move for directions within 30 days after service of the notice of appearance, the objector may move for directions.

Revocation of certificate of appointment

75.04 On the application of any person appearing to have a financial interest in an estate, the court may revoke the certificate of appointment of the estate trustee where the court is satisfied that,

(a) the certificate was issued in error or as a result of a fraud on the court;

(b) the appointment is no longer effective; or

(c) the certificate should be revoked for any other reason.

Return of certificate

Motion for Return of Certificate

75.05 (1) The court may, on motion, order that a certificate of appointment be returned to the court where,

(a) the moving party seeks a determination of the validity of the testamentary instrument for which the certificate was issued or of the entitlement of the estate trustee to the certificate; or

(b) an application has been made under rule 75.04.

Notice

(2) The motion may be made without notice unless the court orders otherwise.

Effect of Order

(3) On service of the order to return the certificate of appointment, the estate trustee shall forthwith deposit the

original certificate with the registrar, and the appointment has no further effect and shall not be acted on until,

(a) the issues referred to in clause (1) (a) or the application referred to in clause (1) (b), as the case may be, have been determined by the court; or

(b) the release of the certificate is ordered under subrule (6).

Motion for Directions

(4) A party who obtains an order under clause (1) (a) shall move for directions under rule 75.06 within 30 days after the making of the order.

(5) The estate trustee may at any time move for directions under rule 75.06 for determination by the court of the matters referred to in clause (3) (a).

Release of Certificate

(6) If a motion for directions referred to in subrule (4) or (5) is not made, the court may, on motion of the estate trustee without notice, order the release to the estate trustee of the certificate of appointment.

Application or motion for directions

75.06 (1) Any person who appears to have a financial interest in an estate may apply for directions, or move for directions in another proceeding under this rule, as to the procedure for bringing any matter before the court.

Service

(2) An application for directions (Form 75.5) or motion for directions (Form 75.6) shall be served on all persons appearing to have a financial interest in the estate, or as the court directs, at least 10 days before the hearing of the application or motion.

Order

(3) On an application or motion for directions, the court may direct,

(a) the issues to be decided;

(b) who are parties, who is plaintiff and defendant and who is submitting rights to the court;

(c) who shall be served with the order for directions, and the method and times of service;

(d) procedures for bringing the matter before the court in a summary fashion, where appropriate;

(e) that the plaintiff file and serve a statement of claim (Form 75.7);

(f) that an estate trustee be appointed during litigation, and file such security as the court directs;

(f.1) that a mediation session be conducted under rule 75.1;

(g) such other procedures as are just.

(4) An order giving directions shall be in Form 75.8 or 75.9.

Procedure where statement of claim served

Defendant: Statement of Defence, Statement of Defence and Counterclaim or Submission of Rights to Court

75.07 (1) Where a statement of claim is delivered as directed under subrule 75.06 (3), each defendant served may serve on each party and file with proof of service,

(a) a statement of defence or a statement of defence and counterclaim; or

(b) a statement of submission of rights to the court (Form 75.10). O. Reg. 484/94, s. 12.

Plaintiff: Reply or Reply and Defence to Counterclaim

(2) A plaintiff may deliver a reply or a reply and defence to counterclaim.

Effect of Failure to File Pleadings

(4) A person who is served with a statement of claim and who does not file a statement of defence, a statement of defence and counterclaim or a statement of submission of rights to the court is not a party to the proceeding and his or her consent to any settlement, agreement or consent judgment is not required.

Submission of rights to court

75.07.1 Where a person files a statement of submission of rights to the court in response to service of a statement of claim or on a motion or application for directions,

(a) the person is not a party to the proceeding and is entitled only to service by the plaintiff of written notice of the time and place of the trial and a copy of the judgment disposing of the matter;

(b) the person is not entitled to costs in the proceeding and is not liable for costs, except indirectly to the extent that costs are ordered to be paid out of the estate; and

(c) a judgment on consent following settlement shall not be given without,

(i) the written consent of the person, or

(ii) an affidavit of a lawyer of record in the proceeding attesting that a notice of settlement (Form 75.11), appended as an exhibit to the affidavit, has been personally served on the person and no rejection of settlement (Form 75.12) has been filed with the court within 10 days after service of the notice...

Claims against an estate

Notice of Contestation of Claim

75.08 (1) A notice of contestation of a claim under section 44 or 45 of the Estates Act shall be in Form 75.13.

Claims

(2) A claim made against an estate under section 44 or 45 of the Estates Act shall be in Form 75.14.

Service

(3) The claimant shall serve the claim on the estate trustee and file the claim and the notice of contestation, with proof of service, within 30 days after service of the notice of contestation on the claimant.

Date of Trial

(4) When the claim and notice of contestation are filed, the registrar shall fix a date for trial.

Manner of Trial

(5) The trial shall proceed in a summary manner unless the judge considers it appropriate to give directions as to the issues, parties and pleadings.

Lawyer of record

75.09 (1) the lawyer who takes any of the following steps on a party's behalf is the party's lawyer of record:

1. Filing a notice of objection under rule 75.03.

2. Moving for return of a certificate under rule 75.05.

3. Moving for directions under rule 75.06. O. Reg. 484/94, s. 12;

(2) Rule 15.02 applies, with necessary modifications, as if the notice or motion were an originating process.

RULE 75.1 MANDATORY MEDIATION – ESTATES, TRUSTS, AND SUBSTITUTE DECISIONS

SCOPE

75.1.02 (1) This Rule applies to proceedings,

(a) that are commenced in, (iii) the City of Ottawa on or after January 1, 2001,

and

(b) to which any of the following applies,

(i) rule 74.18 (application to pass accounts), if the application is contested,

(ii) rule 75.01 (formal proof of testamentary instrument), 75.03 (objection to issuing certificate of appointment), 75.05 (return of certificate) or 75.08 (claims against an estate),

(iii) Part V of the Succession Law Reform Act,

(iv) the Substitute Decisions Act, 1992,

(v) the Absentees Act, the Charities Accounting Act, the Estates Act, the Trustee Act or the Variation of Trusts Act,

(vi) subrule 14.05 (3), if the matters at issue relate to an estate or trust, or

(vii) subsection 5 (2) of the Family Law Act.

(2) The fact that an estate or trust is a party to a proceeding, by virtue of an order to continue under rule 11 or otherwise, is not sufficient to bring the proceeding under this Rule.

Directions for conduct of mediation

Motion for Directions

75.1.05 (1) In a proceeding described in subrule 75.1.02 (1), except a contested passing of accounts under rule 74.18, the applicant shall make a motion, in the same way as under rule 75.06, seeking directions for the conduct of the mediation.

(2) The notice of motion shall be served within 30 days after the last day for serving a notice of appearance.

(3) The motion may be combined with a motion under rule 75.06.

Directions

(4) On the hearing of the motion under this rule, the court may direct,

(a) the issues to be mediated;

(b) who has carriage of the mediation and who shall respond;

(c) within what times the mediation session shall take place;

(d) which parties are required to attend the mediation session in person, and how they are to be served.

(e) whether notice is to be given to parties submitting their rights to the court under rule 75.07.1;

(f) how the cost of the mediation is to be apportioned among the designated parties; and

(g) any other matter that may be desirable to facilitate the mediation.

(5) In a contested passing of accounts the court shall, on the hearing date specified in the notice of application, deal with the matter as if subrule (4) applied.

Non-Compliance

(6) If there is non-compliance with a direction given under subrule (4) or (5), the matter shall be referred,

(b) in the City of Ottawa ... to a judge or a case management master.

www.ingramcontent.com/pod-product-compliance
Lightning Source LLC
Chambersburg PA
CBHW071459200326
41519CB00019B/5806